NEW SOUTH WALES
SYDNEY

Above: Glittering night-time Sydney and its Opera House, reflected in Sydney Harbour. Opposite: Tall ships still sail into Sydney Harbour. This is "Svanen", with the Opera House in the background.

Around 570 species of fish are recorded from the Harbour.

Sydney Harbour Bridge, symbol of a city.

Celebrations merit spectacular fireworks from the Bridge.

SPARKLING SYDNEY HARBOUR
A city's playground

Officially named Port Jackson, this magnificent harbour covers about fifty-four square kilometres and has a shoreline of around 240 kilometres. "The finest harbour in the world", as Captain Phillip described it in 1788, is protected from the waters of the Tasman Sea by North and South Heads. It is Sydney's playground, a place to sail or powerboat, to swim or dive, to windsurf, to fish, or just to admire the view. Fringed with parks, the harbour offers wide expanses, quiet backwaters and protected sandy beaches. Ferries, hydrofoils, yachts, cargo ships and ocean liners can all be seen on its waters.

Looking across the Spit Bridge at Mosman and Middle Harbour to Sydney Harbour entrance.

Above: An aerial view across the seacliffs of the Gap to Watsons Bay, Sydney Harbour and the city. Above inset: Sydney seen from the east, across the marina at Rushcutters Bay.

On weekends, the Harbour is alive with yachts from marinas such as this one at Rushcutters Bay.

Above: The city can be seen in the distance over Point Piper and Darling Point. Above inset: Bathers on Camp Cove Beach, where white people first went ashore at Sydney.

Sailboats of all sizes can be seen on Sydney Harbour.

"I know that the task would be hopeless were I to attempt to make others understand the beauty of Sydney Harbour... The sea runs up in various bays and coves, indenting the land all around the city so as to give a thousand different aspects to the water... water always with jutting corners of land beyond it and then again of water and then again of land."　　ANTHONY TROLLOPE (1873)

"Sydney is one of the places which, when a man leaves it knowing he will never return, he cannot leave without a pang and a tear. Such is its loveliness."　IBID

The Sydney Harbour ferry "Charlotte" crosses Sydney Cove.

Right above: A white wake traces across Sydney Harbour to Circular Quay, between the Opera House and the Harbour Bridge. The Royal Botanic Gardens are in the picture's centre and left. Government House stands behind the Opera House.
Right below: A view over North Sydney to Sydney Harbour, spanned by the Harbour Bridge, and the city centre.

Manly Cove, with Sydney Harbour in the foreground, the Tasman Sea in the background.

A view from Dobroyd Head to South Head on the left and Lady Bay, Camp Cove and Watsons Bay on the right.

Inset above: The cliffs of the Gap and part of Sydney Harbour National Park lead northwards to South Head.

Inset above: Looking across North Head to the Harbour entrance and South Head.
Following pages: Day or night, the massive span of the Harbour Bridge dominates the Sydney waterfront.

Harbour Bridge and Opera House on a misty morning

SYDNEY HARBOUR BRIDGE
A stunning steel span

After completion in 1932, the Harbour Bridge spanned the 500 metres of water between the Rocks' Dawes Point and North Sydney's Milson Point. The highest part of the arch rises 134 metres above the water, the deck is forty-nine metres wide and the massive steel structure may carry 15,000 vehicles per hour at times of peak traffic.

Left: Sydney Harbour, the Harbour Bridge and jewelled Sydney city at night.
Following pages: Sydney Harbour Bridge and Sydney Opera House.

Sunset lights Pier One (right) and the southeastern pylon of Sydney Harbour Bridge.

Sydney Harbour Bridge seen over Kirribilli Head, Admiralty House and Kirribilli House.

"Moonlight Sonata" - a night-time view of Sydney Opera House.

The Opera House, in front of the Royal Botanic Gardens, with Circular Quay to its right.

SYDNEY OPERA HOUSE
A home to all performing arts

Sydney's renowned Opera House, with its soaring roof shells, stands on Bennelong Point, on the eastern side of Sydney Cove, looking landward to the Royal Botanic Gardens and seaward to the glorious Harbour. In the early 1950s, a world-wide competition attracted 233 opera-house designs from 32 countries. Jorn Utzon's vision took fourteen years to build, cost $102 million and was opened by Queen Elizabeth II on 10 October 1973. Today a venue for all performing arts, the Opera House has four main theatres, the Concert Hall, Opera Theatre, Drama Theatre and Music Room.

Right: "Firebird" - the Sydney Opera House against the glow of sunset.

Top: Kings Cross is famous for night-time action and non-stop entertainment. Below inset: The El Alamein Fountain, a landmark in Sydney's Kings Cross.

SYDNEY NIGHTLIFE
Celebrating a sophisticated city

Sydney is a wonderful place after dark, with theatres, restaurants and clubs catering for all tastes. Kings Cross, the city's most densely populated district, is one of the famous nightlife districts of the world. Named after King Edward VII, "the Cross" offers restaurants, discos, nightclubs, specialty shops and the sunburst El Alamein Fountain. "Chinatown", which is centred on Dixon Street, has a variety of great restaurants. The Rocks re-creates colonial life. The Sydney Entertainment Centre presents the world's best artists. Suburbs such as Darlinghurst and Paddington attract diners with a variety of cuisines, the city centre has restaurants galore and for a wide choice of places to eat there's always Darling Harbour ...

Some of the world's best Chinese restaurants are to be found in Sydney's Chinatown.

SYDNEY'S TOWER OF GOLD
The city's tallest structure

The Sydney Tower at Centrepoint is situated in the centre of the city and, at 324.8 metres, is the tallest building in Australia. The Tower has been designed to withstand hurricane-force winds, with a shaft made of forty-six separate prefabricated barrel units of high-strength steel. Each cable weighs about seven tonnes. Access to the turret is by high-speed lifts and two stairways. Four levels of the turret are open to the public. The first level features a revolving *à la carte* restaurant, the second level offers restaurant and bar facilities and the third and fourth have observation facilities.

Above: Icons of two eras: Sydney Tower at Centrepoint and a statue of Queen Victoria.
Right: Sydney skyline displays Sydney Tower at Centrepoint behind the monorail Harbourlink.

DARLING HARBOUR
World by the water

Darling Harbour is one of Sydney's outstanding attractions. Occupying fifty-four hectares, it is easily accessible by walking across the Pyrmont Bridge, by road or ferry, or by a monorail system which links all major attractions in the complex and its four car parks with the city and major bus and rail systems. The Harbourside Shopping Complex offers fifty-four waterfront restaurants and eateries and a stunning array of boutiques and specialty shops.

Left: Swans fly high in the Crystal Galleria over the waterside entrance to the superb Harbourside complex.

Opposite: The Harbourside Festival Marketplace of Darling Harbour is magnificent at night.

Below: The Sydney skyline at night seen over Darling Harbour. In the centre of the picture, the monorail runs over Pyrmont Bridge, passing the Sydney Aquarium.

The popular Exhibition Centre at Darling Harbour covers 25,000 square metres of column-free space.

The stunning Chinese Garden at Darling Harbour, largest of its type outside mainland China.

Sydney Aquarium presents Australia's aquatic life to the world.

The Aquarium takes visitors on a journey through the world of water.

DARLING HARBOUR
Adventures for everyone

At Darling Harbour there is a wide variety of open-air entertainment, including street theatre and music of all kinds. The Australian National Maritime Museum offers nautical history and maritime displays, while the magnificent Chinese Garden, with its exquisite landscapes, is well worth a visit. Sydney Aquarium, dedicated to presenting Australian aquatic life, is one of the world's great aquariums. There is a Convention Centre and an Exhibition Centre the size of three football fields. Nearby, the Powerhouse Museum, created from the shell of an old power station, allows visitors to imagine the future, interact with the present and re-discover the past.

Following pages: Cunard cruise ship leaving the passenger dock at Circular Quay.

Pyrmont Bridge carries a monorail and offers pedestrian access from Darling Harbour to the city centre. At the left is the Sydney Aquarium.

The formal quadrangle of Sydney University.

The opulent foyer of Sydney's historic State Theatre.

The Old Mint, Macquarie Street, was designed by Francis Greenway.

Above: The imposing, colonnaded, Doric facade of the Art Gallery of New South Wales.
Far left: Stately Sydney Town Hall was opened on 27 November 1889.

A CITY'S STATELY BUILDINGS
Statements in stone

Sydney's first Governor, Captain Arthur Phillip, made a plan for the future city which featured spacious streets which were to be sixty metres wide. However, the plan was not realised and in ensuing years streets tended to follow paths of least resistance. It was left to Governor Lachlan Macquarie to take the city in hand and to implement a building programme which took full advantage of the talents of emancipist architect Francis Greenway. In Sydney today, beautifully restored nineteenth-century buildings have been joined by more modern highrise constructions. It is a lovely city, where history has not been forgotten and facades of warm Hawkesbury sandstone glow amongst glittering, glazed towers.

THE QUEEN VICTORIA BUILDING
Restored to splendour

In 1810, Governor Macquarie set aside a site for a market place. In 1828, architect Francis Greenway's Market-house was converted into what became the Central Police Court, while the surrounding area became a Market Square. In 1869, the Market was roofed and the street became an arcade. In 1893, work commenced on the George Street Markets, which, re-named the Queen Victoria Markets Building, was opened five years later. Restoration of the old building began in 1983, and the Queen Victoria Building was reopened in 1986. Today, the Building epitomises the grandiose style of late Victorian architecture and is a fascinating fashion centre, with cafes and restaurants, boutiques and seven-days-a-week shopping.

Top: The awesome Queen Victoria Building occupies an entire city block.
Above inset: Stained-glass windows in the Queen Victoria Building.
Opposite: the interior of the splendidly-renovated Queen Victoria Building.

The Waterfront Restaurant is in a splendidly restored harbourside building in the Rocks.

The Orient Hotel on George Street in the Rocks is one of many places offering hospitality.

THE ROCKS
Where Sydney began

Working parties of convicts from the First Fleet in 1788 cleared the area which gained the name "the Rocks" because of its sandstone outcrops. It became Sydney's earliest commercial and maritime centre, packed with warehouses and taverns and enjoyed by seafarers from all round the world. Today, the Rocks is famous for historic buildings, and a home for Australian arts and crafts. There are also pubs and restaurants, all-Australian entertainment with bush bands and sheep shearing, a Geological and Mining Museum and a Museum of Contemporary Art.

Left: Busy George Street runs through the Rocks towards Sydney Harbour Bridge.

This sculpture in the Rocks Square, Playfair Street, celebrates the colony's early days.

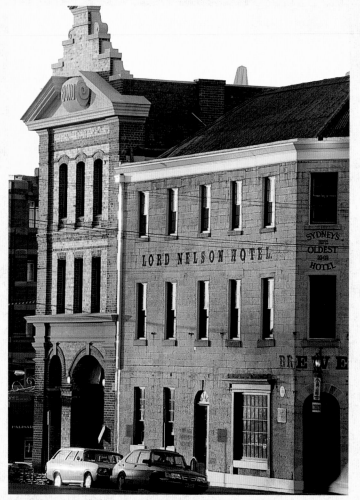

"Sydney's oldest hotel", the Lord Nelson in the Rocks.

Above: Restored bond houses. Right: The "Bounty" replica moored at Circular Quay.

Every pathway in the Royal Botanic Gardens leads to fascinating discoveries.

The Royal Botanic Gardens provide tranquillity in the heart of a busy city.

SYDNEY'S GARDENS
Oases in the city

The area known at the time as the Government Domain was settled upon the people of Sydney by Governor Phillip. Today, the Government Domain has become the magnificent Royal Botanic Gardens. Other city "breathing spaces" include Hyde Park, Prince Alfred Park, Moore Park and superb Centennial Park. On a larger scale is Ku-ring-gai Chase National Park, to the north of the city. South of Sydney the Royal National Park offers splendid coastal scenery.

Above: Spring flowers at Curracurrang, Royal National Park.
Left: A bronze mare and foal, a tribute to the horses of colonial Australia, stand in Sydney's Royal Botanic Gardens.

Taronga offers fascinating glimpses into animal behaviour.

ZOO WITH A VIEW
Taronga on the Harbour

T aronga Zoo's waterfront location, which it has occupied since 1916, is unique, and visitors can admire the animals while appreciating superb Harbour views. Taronga successfully breeds many species, playing a significant role in conservation. The Zoo offers the public many opportunities to learn more about animals and their behaviour through displays such as the Seal Show.

Left: Taronga's elephants have a fine view of Sydney Harbour.

Taronga, with its magnificent site on the shores of Sydney Harbour, is home to many Australian and exotic animals.

FASCINATING WILDLIFE
Australia's animals on show

A short drive west of Sydney city is fascinating Featherdale Wildlife Park, where Australian wildlife, including koalas, kangaroos, wombats and a multitude of brilliant birds, meets the visitor in environmentally integrated settings. Featherdale is noted for breeding Australian animals, with success stories in this field including the first breeding of the White-breasted Sea-eagle.

Right: Eastern Grey Kangaroo and joey.

The Koala, everyone's favourite Australian, can be seen at Featherdale Wildlife Park.

Surf lifesavers competing at a lifesaving carnival.

BONDI BEACH

Bondi, that famous "one thousand metres of golden sand", is the closest ocean beach to Sydney. The beach once called "Bundi" is now known world-wide and is the most popular of a line of great surfing beaches that stretches south to Botany Bay and includes Bronte, Tamarama, Coogee and Maroubra. Bondi's Surf Lifesaving Club was founded in 1906 and is one of the oldest in Australia. Today's volunteer lifesavers carry out surf rescues; they also stage immensely popular carnivals, which showcase the skills of the traditional belt and reel and surfboat teams, but also demonstrate more modern methods of retrieving distressed swimmers. Bondi is the finish-point of the popular annual City-To-Surf Fun-Run.

Right: Bondi Beach with Ben Buckler in the foreground, city skyline in distance.

Bondi Beach is famous around the world for sunshine and surf.

Above: Sunshine, sparkling sea and sand attract crowds to Manly Beach.

Right: Freshwater (foreground) and Manly Beaches, with entrance to Sydney Harbour at top right.

MANLY BEACH
Close to the city, far from care

Manly has two faces. One is the sheltered harbour beach at Manly Cove, reached in half an hour by ferry and less by JetCat from Circular Quay. The second is Manly Beach, whose rolling surf is just a short walk away across the isthmus that separates Sydney Harbour from the Tasman Sea. Four days before the First Fleet anchored at Sydney Cove, Captain Arthur Phillip gave the cove its unusual name because of the "manly bearing" of the Aborigines he met there. It was at Manly, in 1902, that newspaper editor William H. Gocher successfully challenged a law that forbade public swimming in daylight hours. Today, Manly is popular for its beaches, its palm-shaded Corso, its restaurants, boutiques and entertainments. Other attractions include Oceanworld, with its fascinating marine displays, and watersports to suit the most energetic.

Take the horsedrawn tram to see the sights of Manly!

Stroll the Corso from Manly Cove to Manly Ocean Beach.

Surf lifesaving is no longer an all-male activity.

COLOURFUL CARNIVALS
To save lives from the sea

A number of aquatic "firsts" are credited to Sydney's beaches. The "Australian crawl" or freestyle was first introduced by the New Hebridean Tommy Tanna at Manly Baths in the 1890s, while public bathing was legal at Manly from 1903. In November of that year, the Sly brothers started Australia's first Life Saving Service at Manly, using an old fishing boat. Nearly one century later, there are 21 surf lifesaving clubs active in the thirty kilometres of "Northern Beaches" which stretch from Manly to North Palm Beach. Ten surf carnivals, hard-fought competitions between clubs, are held on the Northern Beaches each year. Freshwater Beach, just north of Manly, was the birthplace of surfboard riding in Australia when, in 1914, Hawaii's Duke Kahanamoku demonstrated a sport which today has grown into a consuming passion for many Australians.

Right: a surf lifesaving carnival enthrals spectators at Freshwater Beach.
Insets left to right: Ready for action at a carnival; modern equipment makes Australia's surf lifesavers extremely efficient; reel-carriers at a carnival; the traditional surf-boat competition tests individual ability and teamwork.

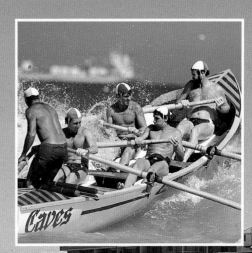

Wollongong Harbour was established by 1844.

WOLLONGONG
Its name means "sound of the sea"

Eighty kilometres south of Sydney, beyond Royal
National Park, Australia's seventh-largest city,
Wollongong, stands on the Illawarra coastal plain. The
name "Wollongong" derives from an Aboriginal word for
"sound of the sea"; from 1844 a harbour here loaded cedar,
then coal. With the development of Port Kembla, south of
the city centre, Wollongong Harbour ceased further
growth. Wollongong is noted for coal and a huge
steelworks, also for its University and for imaginative civic
developments, including lovely gardens, a City Mall, a
fine Library and a noteworthy Performing Arts Centre.

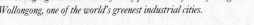

Above: Wollongong's harbour has a fleet of pleasure craft and fishing boats.
Left: Wollongong, one of the world's greenest industrial cities.

THE CENTRAL COAST
Getting away from it all

North of Sydney lies the Central Coast, a short journey over a fast freeway which offers glimpses of sandstone ravines, river estuaries and the ocean. A diversion from the freeway through Gosford, at the head of Brisbane Water, leads to a succession of golden beaches such as Copacabana and Avoca, then to the resort town of Terrigal. A short distance north is The Entrance, guarding the opening to beautiful Tuggerah Lake.

Above: Pearl Beach, a secluded gem on the Central Coast.
Left: Gosford, centre of the Central Coast, stands at the head of Brisbane Water.
Above left: insets left to right: Terrigal, a popular beach resort; The Entrance;
bridge at The Entrance.
Following pages: The Three Sisters, a famed landmark in the Blue Mountains west of Sydney.

Avoca Beach, focus of the Erina Peninsula of the Central Coast.

The Katoomba Scenic Skyway allows superb views of the Jamison Valley.

THE BLUE MOUNTAINS
Scenic splendour and wildlife

The wonderland of sandstone cliffs and ridges, forested gullies, waterfalls and wildlife that is the Blue Mountains is only just over sixty kilometres west of Sydney. The mountains contain a number of charming towns from which to discover the magnificent scenery and abundant wildlife, to bushwalk or rockclimb, to admire some of the beautiful gardens open to the public, or to visit antique shops and art galleries (including artist Norman Lindsay's house at Springwood).

Left: The charming mountain town of Katoomba makes a fine base from which to view the Blue Mountains.
Top left: insets left to right: Victoria Falls; The Blue Mountains are ideal for family holidays: a walkway gives access to one of the Three Sisters.

The King Parrot is common in the Blue Mountains.

· The Early History of ·
SYDNEY
NEW SOUTH WALES

In January 1788, an expedition of over 1300 people, more than 750 of them convicts, arrived from England at a place on the east coast of Australia inhabited for many thousands of years by Aborigines.

Governor Arthur Phillip established a settlement on the Tank Stream, Sydney Cove, on the shores of Port Jackson. By July 1788, Phillip had prepared a plan for the future development of Sydney, with wide streets "to admit free circulation of air".

By 1792, the colony's population was only a little over 3000, but settlements were flourishing at Rose Hill and Parramatta. During the following eight years, the colony was ruled by the military, and then by Governor Hunter, who replaced wooden buildings with new ones of brick and stone. Development under Governors King and Bligh was rapid, and by 1810 there were over 10,000 souls in the colony.

Macquarie, who became Governor in 1810, believed that Sydney would become "as fine and opulent a town as any one in His Majesty's ... dominions". His appointment of architect Francis Greenway helped achieve this object, during a period of economic growth that was helped by the crossing of the Blue Mountains in 1813.

Transportation to New South Wales continued until 1840, by which time over 80,000 convicts had made their contributions to the colony.

Sydney continued to grow steadily and was a considerable city when, on 12 February 1851, Edward Hargraves discovered gold at Summer Hill Creek, near Bathurst. The prosperity that followed led to responsible self-government for New South Wales and began the rise of this harbourside metropolis to today's pre-eminence as one of the world's truly great cities.